# SCIENCE WORLD

# ELECTRICITY
## AND MAGNETISM

### KATHRYN WHYMAN

Franklin Watts
London • Sydney

© Archon Press Ltd 2003

Produced by
Archon Press Ltd
28 Percy Street
London W1T 2BZ

New edition first published in
Great Britain in 2003 by
Franklin Watts
96 Leonard Street
London EC2A 4XD

Original edition published as
Simply Science – Electricity and
Magnetism

ISBN: 0–7496–4964–X

Author: Kathryn Whyman

Design: Phil Kay

Editor: Nicola Cameron

Picture Research: Brian Hunter
Smart

Illustrator: Louise Nevett

Printed in UAE

# CONTENTS

# INTRODUCTION

Telephones, stereo systems and videos all rely on the the power of electricity and magnetism to make them work. Yet many of the electrical devices that we depend on have only been invented in the last century. In fact, people often think of electricity itself as an invention, something 'man-made'. This book looks at how electricity and magnetism are closely related. It explains how together they produce the electric current which we use every day to provide heat, light and power.

Electricity occurs in nature, as seen in the Northern Lights.

Electricity also occurs in nature, in a wide variety of forms. Lightning, electric fish, the Northern Lights, magnetic rocks and the sending of electrical signals in the human brain are just a few examples.

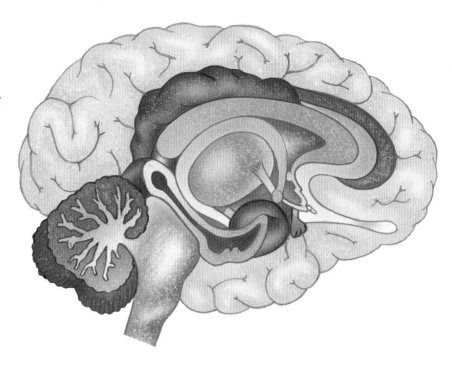

A human brain

# A WORLD WITHOUT ELECTRICITY

Many parts of the world still do not enjoy a constant and everyday supply of electricity. Yet most of us take it for granted, turning switches on and off to power our lights, kettles and televisions. It is hard to imagine a world without an electricity supply. But only a hundred years ago, people used gas, oil or candles to light their homes.

Today, whether for survival, for communications, to save time or for entertainment, an electric supply is an essential part of everyday life.

Life without an electricity supply – washing clothes by hand.

Louiseville, Kentucky, USA – ablaze with lights

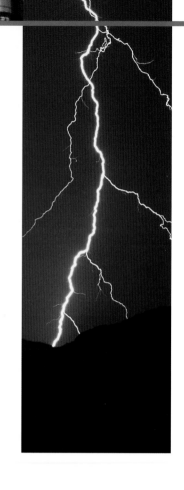

# ELECTRICITY OCCURS NATURALLY

Electricity occurs naturally when certain materials are rubbed together. If you rub a blown-up balloon against a sweater, it makes a type of electricity, or electric charge, called 'static electricity'. The balloon can now pull things towards itself such as pieces of paper and a thin stream of water from a tap.

A dramatic example of electricity occurs naturally when lightning strikes. Lightning is caused by huge amounts of electric charge jumping through the air from cloud to cloud, or to the Earth. This electric charge builds up as drops of water hit hailstones in the clouds. One flash of lightning can be seen for many kilometres. It can destroy trees, start fires, damage buildings and even kill people.

Sparks of static electricity

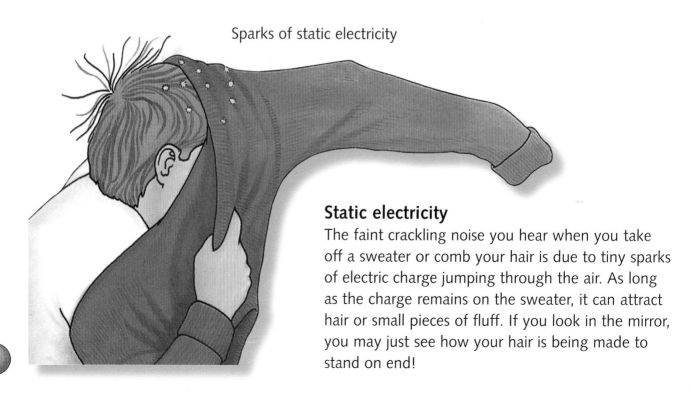

### Static electricity
The faint crackling noise you hear when you take off a sweater or comb your hair is due to tiny sparks of electric charge jumping through the air. As long as the charge remains on the sweater, it can attract hair or small pieces of fluff. If you look in the mirror, you may just see how your hair is being made to stand on end!

Huge amounts of electric charge jump through the air from these clouds in Texas, USA.

Electricity occurs naturally when lightning strikes. Occasionally, lightning may strike an object.

# MAGNETIC EARTH

Two thousand years ago, the Chinese discovered a special black stone. When a small splinter of this stone was hung on a thread, it always pointed in the same direction. We call this kind of stone a 'lodestone', and the direction it points is always north-south.

Anything which behaves in the same way as a lodestone is called a magnet. A compass needle is simply a tiny magnet. All magnets exert a force around them, and their lines of force make up a 'magnetic field'. The Earth itself is like a giant magnet and is also surrounded by its own magnetic field.

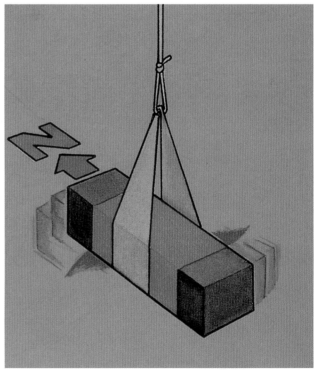

## Magnetic fields

The magnetism of the Earth is shown as lines of force making up its magnetic field. These lines are drawn between the North Pole and the South Pole.

The end of the magnet which points towards the Earth's North Pole is also called the north pole of the magnet. The other end is called the south pole of the magnet.

# USING A COMPASS

A map is very useful to a traveller but it does not tell you in which direction you are facing. You can find this out by using a compass. The compass needle is affected by the Earth's magnetic field and always points northwards. The map can then be lined up with the compass. In fact, a compass needle does not point to the geographical or true North Pole. It points to the magnetic north, a point in Northern Canada, 1,600km away from the true North Pole.

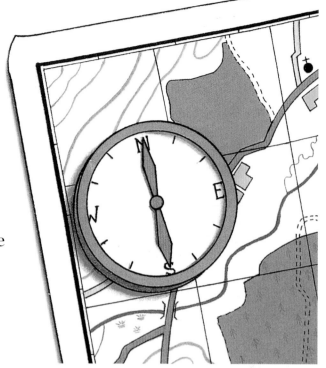

A map and compass will help you find which direction you are facing.

# MORE ABOUT MAGNETS

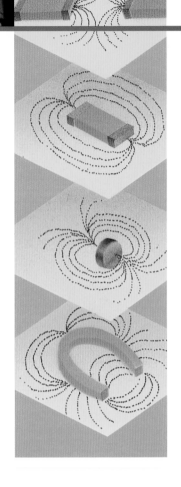

Pointing to the north is only one of the many things a magnet can do. Magnets exert a force on almost anything in their magnetic field. Usually, this force is very weak. But if two magnets are held together so that the north pole of one faces the south pole of the other, the magnets will pull towards each other.

A piece of steel can be easily magnetised by stroking it several times in the same direction with a magnet. A steel magnet is called a 'permanent' magnet because it can often keep its magnetic powers for a long time.

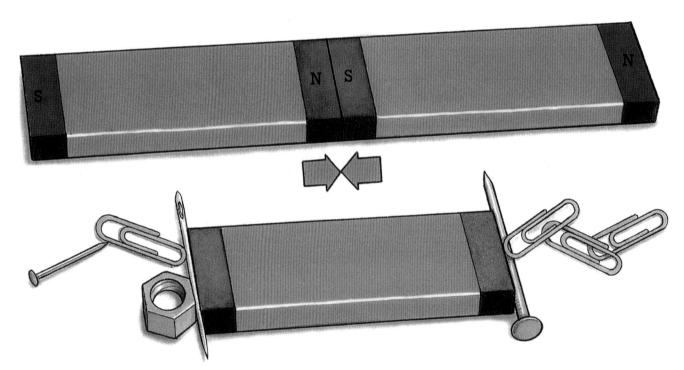

### Attracting opposite poles

The north and south poles of a magnet are described as opposite poles. If opposite poles of two magnets are placed near each other they 'attract'.

### Attracting metals

Small iron or steel objects, like pins and paper clips, will be attracted to the magnet. The attraction is strongest at each of the magnet's poles.

# MAGNETIC HOVERING TRAINS

Magnets have another interesting property. If they are held so that like poles are facing, they will push each other away, or *repel*. This principle can be seen at work in a special magnetic hovering train. Powerful magnets placed beneath the train all have their north poles facing down towards the track. The track itself also has magnets in it.

These magnets have their north poles facing up towards the train. Because the north poles repel each other, the train is lifted off the track. It can now glide along the track with ease. The magnets used by the magnetic train are not permanent – they only attract and repel when electricity flows through them. Magnets like these are called 'electromagnets'.

A magnetic hovering train in Taejon, South Korea

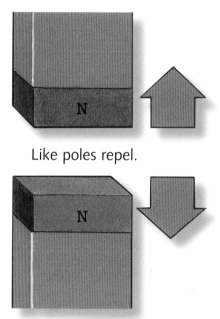

Like poles repel.

# ELECTROMAGNETS

Electricity and magnetism are very closely related. Another way of making a magnet is to pass electricity through a wire wrapped around a metal core, usually iron. The iron core becomes an 'electromagnet'. Smaller electromagnets are used in the home; look inside an electric doorbell and you will see an electromagnet shaped like a horse-shoe with wires wrapped around its arms. Large electromagnets are used in magnetic hovering trains (see page 13).

Powerful electromagnets are often used in scrapyards and can lift heavy loads. Because magnets only attract a few metals, they can be used to separate one kind of metal from another.

## A simple electromagnet

When electricity flows through the wire, the nail, now an electromagnet, can pick up paper clips. An electromagnet is not a permanent magnet – once the iron core loses its magnetism the paper clips drop.

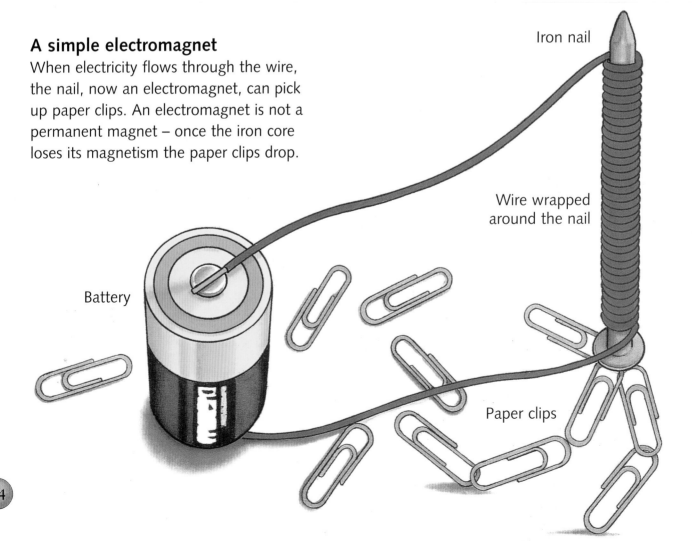

Iron nail

Wire wrapped around the nail

Battery

Paper clips

An electromagnetic crane is used to lift scrap iron and steel.

# MAKING AN ELECTRIC CURRENT

Electricity occurs naturally as static electricity. But static electricity is the sudden and uncontrollable movement of an electric charge. It cannot be used very easily to drive machines. Many machines are driven by an 'electric current', the controlled movement of an electric charge.

Electricity can make magnets, and magnets can make, or 'generate', an electrical current. A bicycle dynamo generates electric current to light up its lamps. In some rural places, people use a petrol or diesel engine to drive a powerful dynamo called a 'generator', to provide their own source of electric current.

**An electric current** can be made to flow through a wire, by moving the wire across a magnetic field. It does not matter if the wire or the magnet moves, so long as one moves in relation to the other. A bicycle dynamo produces an electric current by using the movement of the wheel to move a magnet within a coil of wire.

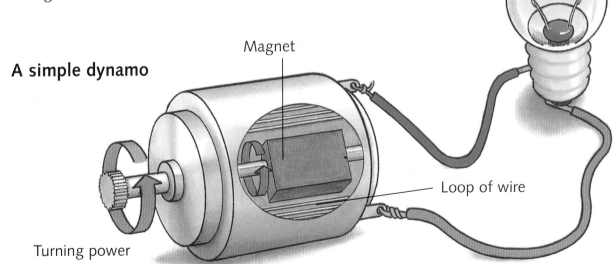

Small light bulb

Magnet

**A simple dynamo**

Loop of wire

Turning power

A small, local generator in China

# POWER STATIONS

Power stations produce electricity on a large scale, for industry, cities and homes. They use giant generators, usually powered by coal, gas, oil or the energy from nuclear reactions. Steam is produced at great pressure to drive a 'turbine'. The turbine is rotated by the force of the steam. In a hydroelectric power station, the turbine is turned by the force of moving water instead of steam. The turbine drives the generator.

There are many different types of generators powered by a variety of sources, but in all of them the electric current is generated by magnets being turned at speed inside coils of wire.

The familiar site of cooling towers at a power station

A series of turbine blades and a generator under construction

# FROM POWER STATIONS TO HOMES

Once the electric current has been generated, it must be carried from the power station to wherever it is needed. Electric current is carried in thick wires called cables. Some are buried beneath the ground and others, supported by pylons are carried high above the ground.

A system of pylons and cables connects all the power stations into one huge network called the 'grid'. The grid can switch power from one area to another, as demand varies. If a power station fails, a local power cut can still be avoided. Electric current from another power station is sent along the cables to keep the power supply in the area.

Pylons carrying cables from the power station

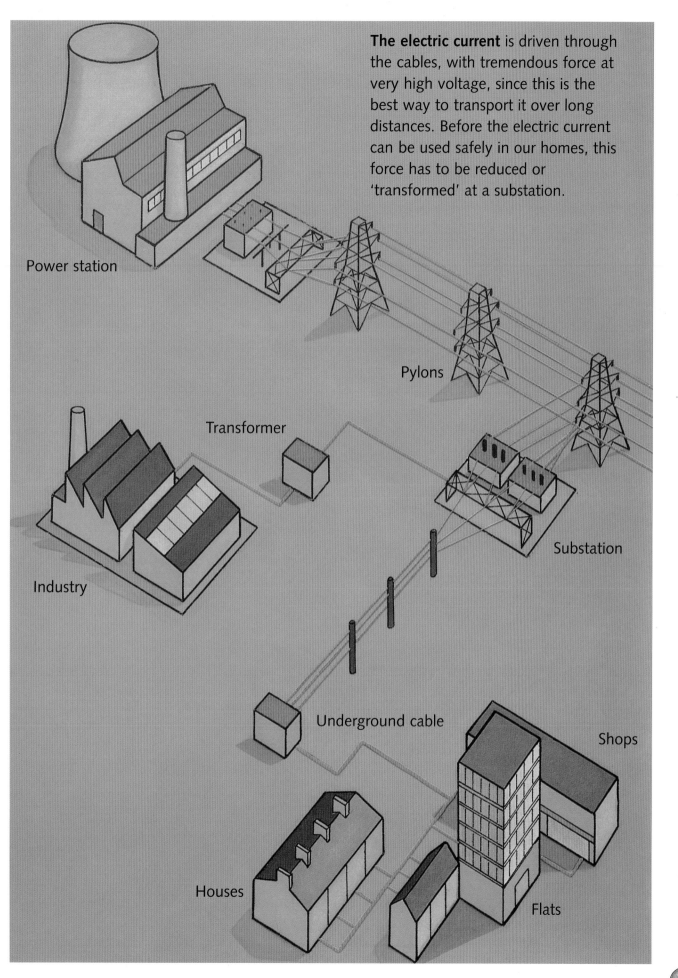

**The electric current** is driven through the cables, with tremendous force at very high voltage, since this is the best way to transport it over long distances. Before the electric current can be used safely in our homes, this force has to be reduced or 'transformed' at a substation.

Power station

Pylons

Transformer

Industry

Substation

Underground cable

Shops

Houses

Flats

# ELECTRICITY TRAVELS IN CIRCUITS

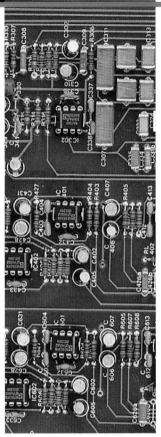

To connect a light bulb to an electricity supply we need two wires. Electric current flows from the power supply, down one wire to the bulb and back along the other wire to the power supply. The path of the electric current is called a 'circuit'. If there are no breaks in the circuit, the current will continue to flow and the bulb will stay lit.

Most electric wires are made of metal strands coated with plastic or rubber. The electric current flows easily through the metal strands but not through the plastic. When the current flows through the wire, the wire becomes *live*.

## A simple circuit

A switch is simply a way of making and breaking a circuit. When a switch is in the 'on' position, an electric current flows through the circuit. As soon as the switch is turned to the 'off' position, the circuit is broken.

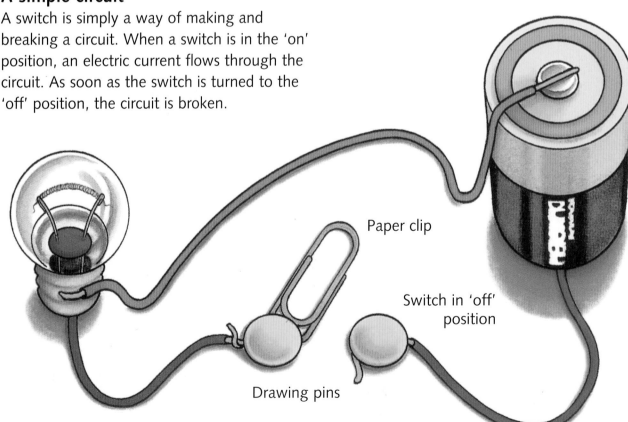

Paper clip

Switch in 'off' position

Drawing pins

# FUSES

A faulty wire can produce enough heat to start a house fire.

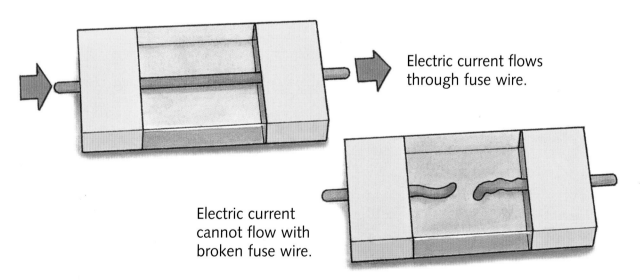

Electric current flows through fuse wire.

Electric current cannot flow with broken fuse wire.

If the wires leading to and from a light bulb touch each other, there is a sudden increase in current flowing through them and they become very hot. This is called a 'short circuit' and can be a fire risk.

To avoid this fire risk, many plugs or circuits are fitted with a fuse – a piece of wire in a circuit which melts as soon as the current is too high. Once the fuse 'blows', the circuit is broken.

# WHAT IS AN ELECTRIC CURRENT?

A wire is made up of millions of tiny particles, too small to see, called atoms. The tiny atom itself is made up of several different parts. Around the centre of the atom, the 'nucleus', particles called electrons are arranged.

**An atom** consists of a nucleus surrounded by electrons moving in orbits. Each electron is a tiny negative charge and is attracted to the positively charged nucleus.

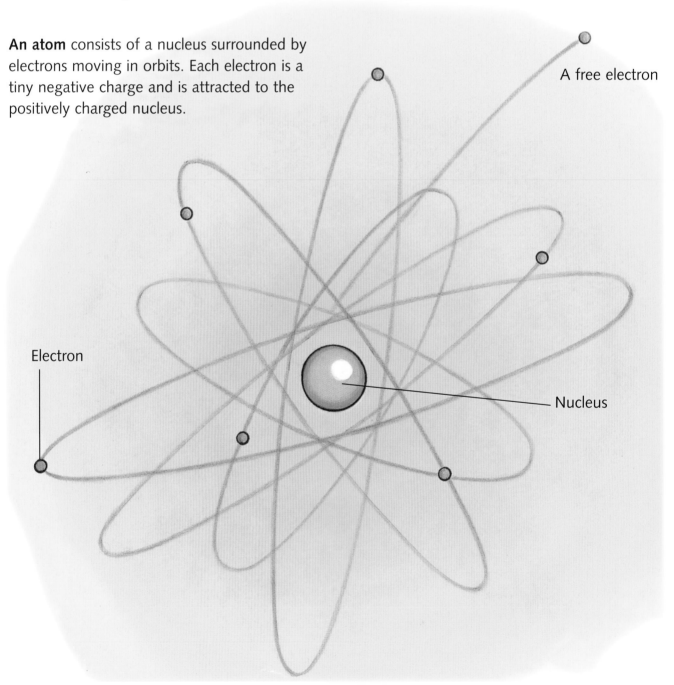

A free electron

Electron

Nucleus

These electrons circle around the nucleus at different distances from it and at great speed. In a metal wire, however, the outer electrons are free to wander at random around the atoms. When a wire is connected to a power supply, like a battery, these free outer electrons are driven in a single direction. Each electron is a tiny negative charge and it is this flow of negative charge which we call an electric current. To make a torch bulb light up for one second takes a flow of about one million, million, million electrons!

**When an electric current** flows, the free outer electrons all move in the same direction. In the very thin wire in a light bulb, the filament, the collisions between the electrons and atoms are more frequent than in an ordinary wire. This increases the temperature of the wire and makes the wire give off heat, which we see as light.

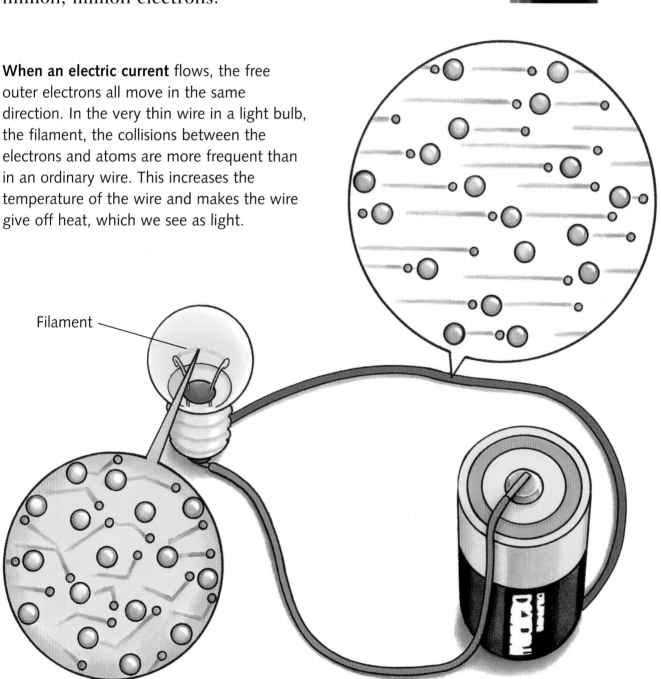

Filament

# BATTERIES

Torches, alarm clocks and other portable appliances need their own power supply and they use batteries. A battery cannot store electricity but it is used to make an electric current when it is needed. Inside the battery are two metal plates, each covered by a chemical. When the battery is connected to a light bulb in a circuit, electrons flow through the chemical from one plate along the wire lighting up the bulb, and back to the other plate.

Batteries come in many different shapes and sizes depending on what they are needed for. Many have to be thrown away once the chemicals have been used up, but others can be 'recharged' and may last a long time.

A battery can be large enough to power a car, or small enough to fit into a watch.

# THE ELECTRIC MOTOR

Many toy cars are powered by an electric motor connected to a battery. An electric motor depends on the same principle as a dynamo: the movement of a wire coil in a magnetic field. In a dynamo, a turning force is used to generate an electric current. However, in the electric motor, a current is used to produce a turning force which drives a shaft connected to the wheels of a car.

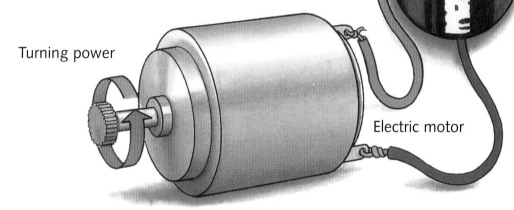

Turning power

Electric motor

Toy cars are often powered by batteries.

# MAKE AN ELECTRO-MAGNETIC CRANE

By following the instructions and diagrams, you can make your own electromagnetic crane. You can use it to pick up small metal objects.

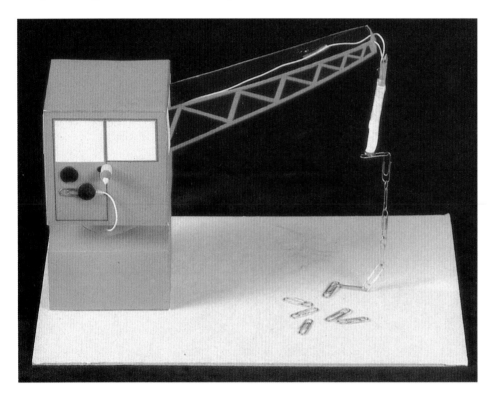

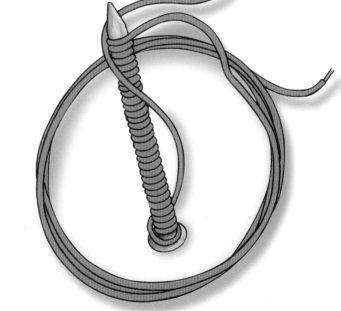

## What you need

An iron nail, a metre of thin plastic coated wire, two boxes, a cotton reel, a pencil, a 1.5V battery, a cardboard tube, some card, two drawing pins, a paper clip, some glue and sticky tape, and scissors.

## Making the electromagnet

Wind the middle part of the wire tightly round the nail, leaving the ends free. One end should be about 20cm longer than the other. When the ends of the wire are connected to the battery, the nail should become a magnet.

## Making the crane

Make the arm by folding a piece of card. Pierce two holes in the end of it. Fix the base of the arm to a cotton reel with glue. Push a pencil through the card and the cotton reel. Remove the pencil and place the cotton reel halfway down the upper box. Make holes in this box for the pencil. Now make slits so the arm can move up and down.

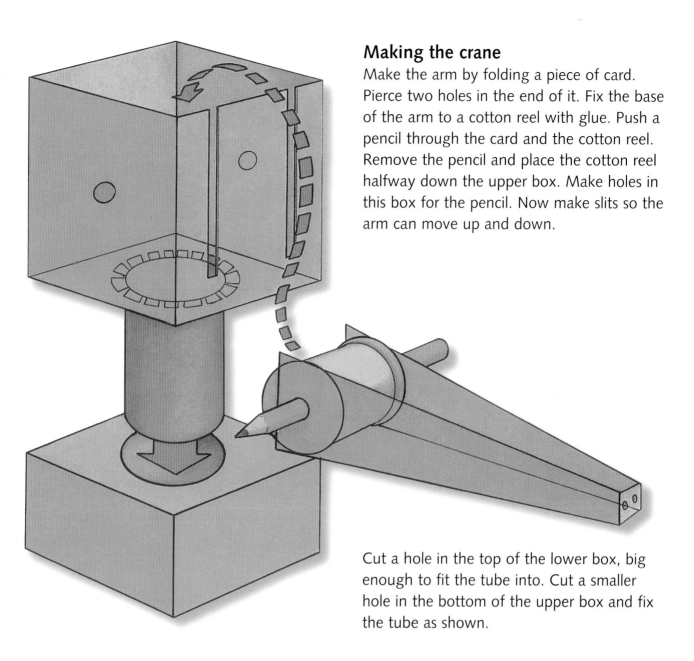

Cut a hole in the top of the lower box, big enough to fit the tube into. Cut a smaller hole in the bottom of the upper box and fix the tube as shown.

## Wiring

Push two drawing pins into the upper box. One should hold a paper clip in position. This acts as a switch. Cut a piece of wire 15cm long from the long end of wire attached to the nail. All the ends of the wires should have their plastic coating removed. Connect the wires with tape as shown in the diagram. Decorate your crane as you choose. When the clip touches both pins, the crane will be ready to use.

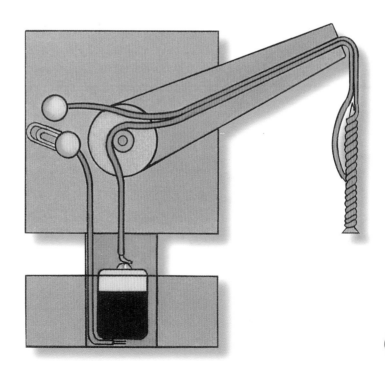

# MORE ABOUT ELECTRICITY

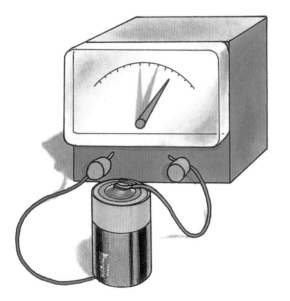

## Measuring an electric current

We can measure how much current is moving through a wire by using an Ammeter. An ammeter is rather like a traffic census counting the number of vehicles driving past a given point on a road. We measure the flow of electrons in Amperes (AMPS). If the current measures one amp, it means that six million, million, million electrons flow past a single point in the wire each second.

## Measuring voltage

The negative terminal of the battery may be very negative in respect to the positive terminal. In this case, electrons are pushed along the wire very hard. We say that the electric current flows with a high voltage. If the negative terminal is weaker, the electrons are pushed more gently. The electric current now has a low voltage. Voltage is measured in units called VOLTS by a Voltmeter.

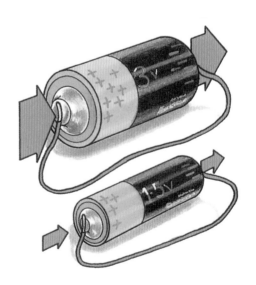

## Watts

If you look on a light bulb, you will see another measurement. These are WATTS, a unit of power. The power of electricity depends on how much current is flowing (its amps) and how hard it is being pushed (its volts). The faster it moves and the harder it is pushed, the greater the power.

# GLOSSARY

### Atom
The smallest particle of any substance. Atoms are made up of a central nucleus surrounded by tiny moving electrons.

### Compass
An instrument used to show directions. It has a magnetic needle that pivots freely and points in a north direction.

### Dynamo
A machine that changes movement (kinetic energy) into electrical energy.

### Electric charge
The amount of electricity held within something. The particles of an atom carry electric charge.

### Electric current
The flow of electrons through a conductor such as copper wire.

### Electromagnet
An iron bar surrounded by a coil of wire. It acts as a magnet when an electric current flows through the wire.

### Hydroelectric
Producing electricity from the energy of moving water.

### Lines of force
The lines along which the force of a magnet acts. Lines of force make up a magnetic field.

### Magnet
A piece of iron that can attract iron or steel. A magnet will attract or repel other magnet. When able to turn, a magnet will always point in a north-south direction.

### Magnetic field
The space around a magnet within which its magnetic force acts.

### Orbit
The path taken by an electron as it circles around the nucleus of an atom.

### Recharge
To build up electrical energy again, once it has been lost. Car batteries, for example, can be recharged once they have gone 'flat'.

### Short circuit
An accidental fault in an electric circuit which reduces or cuts off the flow of electricity.

### Static electricity
An electric charge that builds up on the surface of materials that do not conduct electricity. Static electricity is caused by friction.

### Voltage
The strength of the electrical force in an electric current, measured in volts.

# *INDEX*

**Photocredits**
Abbreviations: l-left, r-right, b-bottom, t-top, c-centre, m-middle
Cover main — Select Pictures. front cover mt, 1, 4-5, 8tr, 9t, 16tr, 18tr, 20b — Corbis. front cover mb, 6b — Corel. 2-3, 6tr, 7 — Photodisc. 4tl, 4tr, 6tl, 8tl, 10tl, 11b, 12tl, 14tl, 16tl, 18tl, 20tl, 22tl, 24tl, 24tr, 26tl, 26tr, 28tl, 30tl, 31tl, 32tl — Brian Hunter Smart. 9b — Digital Stock. 10tr, 26br — R. Vlitos. 13, 20tr — Flat Earth. 14tr, 22tr, 25tr, 30tr — Ingram Publishing. 15, 28tr — Barnaby's. 17 — Peter Fraenkel. 18b — Tony Stone. 19 — CEGB. 23 — FEMA. 26bl — Spectrum. 27b — Robert Harding.